Make and Use

Shoes
& Slippers

Anna-Marie D'Cruz

WAYLAND

First published in 2007
by Wayland

© Copyright 2007 Wayland

Wayland
338 Euston Road
London NW1 3BH

Wayland Australia
Level 17/207 Kent Street
Sydney NSW 2000

Senior Editor: Jennifer Schofield
Designer: Jason Billin
Project maker: Anna-Marie D'Cruz
Photographer: Chris Fairclough
Proofreader: Susie Brooks

Acknowledgements:
The Publishers would like to thank the following models:
Emel Augustin, Ammar Duffus, Jade Campbell, Akash Kohli,
Ellie Lawrence, Adam Menditta and Eloise Ramplin

Picture Credits:
All photography Chris Fairclough except
page 4 top: Eddie Keogh/Reuters/CORBIS; page 4
bottom: Christoph Sagel/zefa/CORBIS; page 5: Stefan
Matzke/NewSport/CORBIS

CIP data
D'Cruz, Anna-Marie
   Shoes and slippers. - (Make and use)
   1. Shoes - Design and construction - Juvenile literature
   I. Title
   685.3'103

ISBN: 978 0 7502 5053 5

Printed in China

Wayland is a division of Hachette Children's Books.

Note to parents and teachers:
The projects in this book are designed to be made by children. However, we do recommend adult supervision at all times as the Publisher cannot be held responsible for any injury caused while making the projects.

Contents

All about shoes

We wear shoes and slippers to keep our feet warm or cool and to protect them from the ground we walk on. Most shoes and slippers have a sole, a heel and an upper part.

PARTS OF A SHOE

The sole is the part of a shoe between the bottom of the foot and the ground. Some shoes have special soles, depending on what they are used for. For example, footballers' boots have studs so that the players do not slip on the grass (see right).

The heel is the part of a shoe below the back of the foot. Heels come in many shapes and sizes. For example, the stiletto is a lady's shoe with a very long, thin heel. Platform boots have thick and chunky heels.

The upper part of a shoe covers the top of the foot. This can be as simple as a few straps, like those of a sandal (see left, middle), or it can be made from leather and have laces that keep the shoe closed (see left).

SHOES FOR SPORTS

People who take part in sports or certain hobbies need to wear special shoes as part of their kit or uniform. Golf shoes, like football boots, have small spikes on their soles. Ballet dancers wear pointe shoes that help them to balance on their toes, and speed skaters wear boots with a blade on the sole that cuts the ice as they skate (see left).

GET STARTED!

This book shows you how to make different types of shoes and slippers from around the world. When you are making your shoes, remember that some materials may not be strong enough to wear outside. Try to use materials that you already have. For the fabric in these projects, old clothes, pillow cases and towels that you no longer use are ideal. Reusing and recycling materials like this is good for the environment and it will save you money. The projects have all been made and decorated for this book but do not worry if yours look a little different – just have fun making and wearing your shoes.

Leaf shoes

Long ago people used leaves, bark and grass to protect their feet. Try these leaf shoes and see how they compare to your trainers.

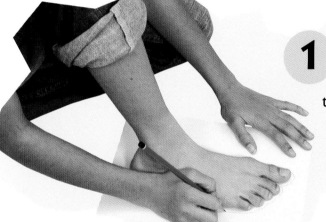

1 Draw around each of your feet onto the card. Cut out the two shapes.

2 Draw lots of different leaf shapes onto the coloured paper. You could copy some of the shapes on the right. Cut out the leaves.

6

3 Glue down the leaves onto the foot-shaped cards. Overlap the leaves and make sure that each foot-shape is completely covered.

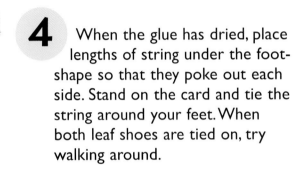

4 When the glue has dried, place lengths of string under the foot-shape so that they poke out each side. Stand on the card and tie the string around your feet. When both leaf shoes are tied on, try walking around.

MATERIAL MATTERS

Think about the materials you have used to make your leaf shoes. How do your feet feel inside them? How much protection does the card offer? If you wanted to wear these shoes outside, what materials would you use to make them?

Roman sandals

Caligae were sandals worn by Roman soldiers. Leather was cut into a laced pattern and tied together over the feet and up the leg above the soldier's ankle. Make these simple sandals and march off as if you are going into battle.

YOU WILL NEED

A3 sheet of thin card
pencil
ruler
pair of scissors
fake leather fabric
hole punch
thin corrugated card
glue
2 long shoe laces

1 To make a template, put your foot on the card and draw around it. Lift your foot off the card and draw in the straps, as shown. Cut out the template.

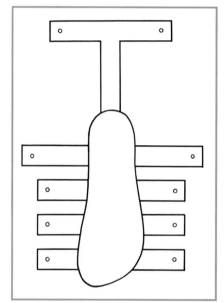

2 Test the template to make sure the straps are long enough and in the right place for your foot. Then draw around the template onto the fabric.

3 Cut out the sandal. Use the hole punch to make holes in the fabric as shown on the template in step 1.

4 Put your foot on the corrugated card and draw around it. Cut out the foot-shape and glue it to the inside of the fabric.

5 Turn over the template and repeat steps 2–4 to make a sandal for the other foot.

6 Put your feet on the shoes and thread the laces through the holes so that the sandals fit snuggly around each foot. Tie the ends of the laces together.

MARCH IN TO BATTLE

The Roman soldiers' sandals were made of tough leather to last through long marches. The design made the shoes comfortable to wear and kept the soldiers' feet cool. The soles were fitted with a type of stud that made the shoes last longer, but the studs were also useful for stamping and injuring enemies in battle.

Funky flip-flops

Flip-flops are similar to the flat-bottomed sandals worn in Japan to keep feet cool in hot weather. They have no fastenings but are held to the feet by plastic, lace or ribbon straps that go between the toes.

YOU WILL NEED

card from cereal packet
pencil
pair of scissors
coloured artfoam
double-sided tape
2 lengths of ribbon 14cm
strong tape
2 lengths of ribbon 30cm

1 Put one foot on the card and draw around it. Add 1cm all the way around and cut out the shape.

2 Use the shape as a template and cut out four more of the same shape from art foam. Stick two of the artfoam shapes together with double-sided tape to make a thick layer – this is the bottom of your flip-flop sole. Stick the cardboard template and the last two shapes together. Make sure that the template is at the bottom. This is the top of the flip-flop sole.

3 Put your foot onto the top of the flip-flop sole. Use a pencil to make a mark between your big toe and second toe. Push a pencil through the mark so that it makes a hole.

4 Make a loop with the shorter piece of ribbon and feed it through the hole from the card side. The loop needs to be long enough to come up between your toes. Stick down the ends of the loop with strong tape.

5 Thread one of the longer ribbons through the loop. Stick one end to the bottom of the card halfway along one side of the flip-flop. Put the flip-flop on and pull the ribbon so that it goes over your foot but is not too tight. Stick the end of the ribbon to the card. Cut off any spare ribbon.

6 Stick the top of the flip-flop sole to the bottom with double-sided tape. Make the second flip-flop by repeating the steps, but use your other foot to make the template.

GETA SANDALS

Japanese Geta sandals, which are usually made from wood, have two separate blocks on the bottom of the shoe to give the women who wear them extra height. This means that they can wear a full-length kimono without the bottom of it getting dirty.

Dutch clogs

The clog, or 'klompen', is a wooden shoe worn in the Netherlands. Clogs are so strong that they have been used as a protective shoe for working in factories, farms and mines.

1 Draw around your foot onto corrugated card. Add 5mm all the way around and cut out the shape. Use this shape as a template. Cut out four more of the same shape from the corrugated card. Glue one on top of the other.

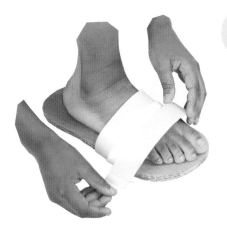

2 To create the arch over the foot, cut strips of card 2cm wide from a cereal box. Using a strip at a time, tape the strip to the bottom of the clog. Curve the strip around your foot and tape it down on the opposite side, under the sole. Keep checking that there is enough room for your foot to foot to fit under the arch.

3 Cut smaller strips of card to cover the top of the foot and toes. Cut a long strip to go around the heel and tape it in place.

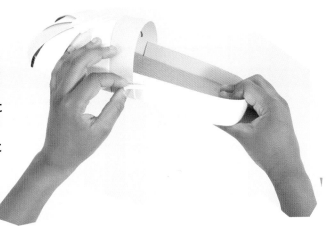

4 Scrunch up rolls of newspaper to wrap around the heel and tape them onto the shoe. Scrunch up a small roll of paper and tape it onto the toe.

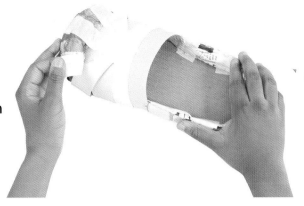

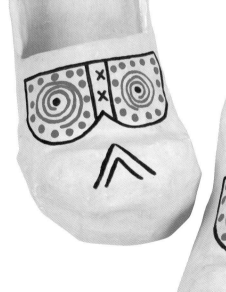

5 Cover your work surface with sheets of newspaper. Use the PVA glue and water mixture to papier mâché the clog with strips of newspaper, covering it completely and building up around the toe and heel to create a clog shape. Finish with a layer of white paper.

6 Repeat steps 1–5 to make the other clog. Allow both to dry.

7 Paint both clogs and leave them to dry. Traditional clogs are often one colour, but you can draw patterns on them if you like.

GET CRAFTY!

Papier mâché can be used to make all sorts of different shapes. All you need is some PVA glue and water mixture and paper. To make the PVA glue and water mixture, dilute about one cup of PVA glue with about a tablespoon of water. The glue should be thinner but not watery. Then take strips of paper, dip them into the glue mixture and stick them onto the framework of whatever you are making. You may need to stick down several layers to make the right shape.

Fun fur boots

The Saami people live in northern Scandinavia in an area known as Lapland. They wear boots made mainly from reindeer skin and fur. These boots will definitely keep your feet warm on a cold winter's night.

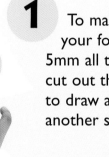

1 To make the sole, draw around your foot onto thick card. Add 5mm all the way round and cut out the shape. Use this shape to draw around and cut out another sole piece.

2 Then cut a strip of card 4cm wide to go around the front of the boot. To tape the strip to the front of the boot, cut 2cm-deep tabs into it. Bend the tabs under the sole and tape them in place.

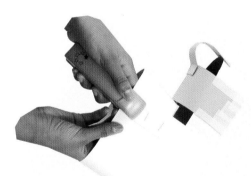

3 Cut a strip of card that is 15cm wide and can go around the back of the boot. As in step 2, cut tabs into the card, bend them under the sole and tape them in place.

4 Add more strips of card to build up the top of the boot and add an upturned strip at the toe. Add strips to give the front of the ankle some height and staple them in place. Keep checking that you can still get your foot in and out of the boot. Glue the spare sole to the bottom.

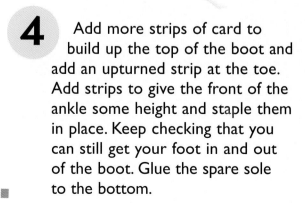

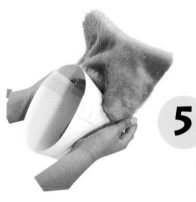

5 Cut out some fake fur and stick it onto the boot to cover the cardboard.

6 Cut a length of felt long enough to go around the ankle of your boot. To decorate the felt, stick different coloured strips of felt and ribbon onto the strip. Pinking shears will give a great effect if you have a pair.

7 Wrap the felt around the ankle of the boot and staple the ends together at the back of the boot. Tape over the staples in the inside of the boots so that they do not hurt you.

8 Repeat the steps to make a boot for your other foot and you will be ready to go off reindeer herding!

Lotus shoes

These shoes, also known as bound-feet shoes, were made for very small feet. In China, big feet were once seen as ugly, so young girls had their feet wrapped in bandages to stop them from growing any longer than 8–10cm.

YOU WILL NEED

thick card
pencil
pair of scissors
thin card
scraps of fabric
sticking tape
glue
corrugated card

1 Draw around your foot onto some stiff card. Add an extra 5mm all around the foot shape. Extend your outline from the toe to a point, and round off the heel to give the shape shown. Cut out the sole shape and use it as a template to cut out another piece of card the same shape.

2 Measure a piece of thin card long enough to go around the sole and 2cm higher than you want your shoe to be. Shape the ends as shown and cut out the shape. Cut the same shape from the fabric, but add an extra 1cm to the top. Set aside the piece of fabric.

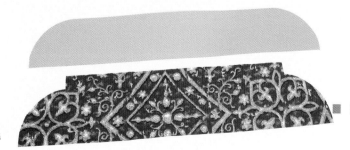

3 Snip tabs along the bottom edge of the card. Then draw in fold lines onto the ends of the card as shown. Using a blunt pencil, go over each fold line quite hard to make a crease.

16

4 Starting at the front of the shoe, bend the tabs around the edge of the sole, taping them down as you go. Glue the curved faces together, one on top of the other.

TINY FEET

Imagine how small your feet would have to be to fit in a shoe 8–10cm in length. What difference would this make to your walking? What other problems do you think small shoes would cause?

5 Tape the fabric cut in step 2 to the outside of your shoe, taping under the shoe and over the rim at the top. Glue the spare card sole to bottom of the shoe.

6 To make the heel, cut out four circles of corrugated card which are as wide as the heel-end of your shoe. Glue one on top of the other.

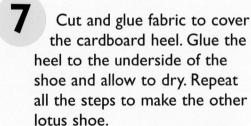

7 Cut and glue fabric to cover the cardboard heel. Glue the heel to the underside of the shoe and allow to dry. Repeat all the steps to make the other lotus shoe.

Jutti slippers

Juttis are worn by women in India. They are worn with sarees and are often decorated with threads and beads. Sometimes the heel is open like this one, but it can also be covered.

YOU WILL NEED

flexible card

pencil

pair scissors

plain coloured fabric

glue

paper

strong sticking tape

stapler

double-sided tape

embroidery thread

sequins

PVA glue

1 Place your foot onto the card and draw around it. Add an extra 5mm around the sole shape and round off the toe end, as shown. Cut out the shape.

2 Draw a second sole as in step 1 but instead of a round toe, make the toe pointy. Cut out the shape and use it as a template to cut out two shapes from the fabric. Glue the fabric to either side of the card. Put this aside to use in step 6.

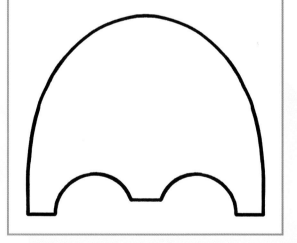

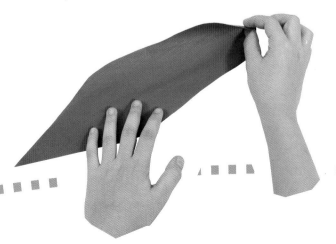

3 To make the upper part of the slipper, draw the shape shown above onto paper. Check that it goes over your foot. Add an extra 2cm all around and cut it out.

4 If the upper shoe shape is wide enough copy it onto some card. Cut it out. Then, cut a piece of fabric in this shape and glue it to the card. Allow the glue to dry.

5 Snip around the outer edge of the upper shoe to make tabs. Place the rounded sole and top piece together with the middle of the toes meeting. Bend and tape the tabs under the slipper's sole.

6 Stick the upper shoe to the pointy sole with double-sided tape. Curl the pointy end over and staple it to the top of the toe piece.

7 Repeat the steps to make a slipper for the other foot.

8 Glue on threads and sequins to decorate the slippers. You could finish them off by adding a tassel or pom-poms.

INDIAN SAREES

A saree is the traditional dress worn by many women in India. It is a very long strip of unstitched fabric that is draped in different ways. The most common style is for the saree to be wrapped around the waist, with one end draped over the shoulder. Sarees are usually worn over a petticoat with a short-sleeved blouse.

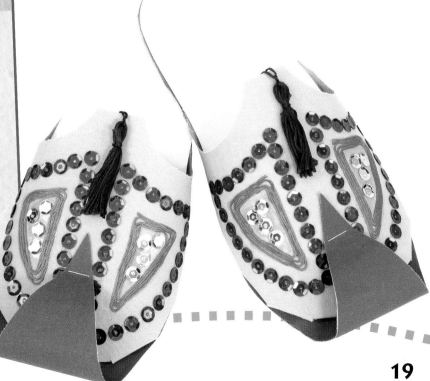

Native American moccasins

The moccasin is a soft slipper made from leather. It was traditionally worn by Native Americans. Some moccasins had hard soles to protect the feet from rough ground. Soft soles were used where the ground was gentler. Often, moccasins are decorated with beads to make patterns and ties.

YOU WILL NEED

thin card
pen
pair of scissors
ruler
2 A3 sized sheets of paper
masking tape
soft fabric
blunt needle
thread
cord
beads
feathers

1 Place your foot in the middle of the card, draw around it and cut it out. Place this template into the middle of an A3 sheet of paper and draw around it, rounding off the toes. Draw and cut out another shape around this as shown, making it 4cm wider around the toe area and 2cm longer at the heel.

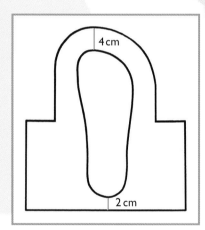

4 cm

2 cm

2 Tape the template to the fabric and cut out the shape.

RUNNING STITCH

To sew a running stitch, start by threading a needle. Tie a knot at the other end of the thread. Push the point of the needle down through the fabric. Bring the needle back up again at a point further forward from where you went down. Repeat this to give a row of stitches that look the same on both sides of the fabric.

3 Cut a template for the toe piece. It should be smaller in width than the sole piece but 2cm wider than your foot. Cut out the pattern and tape it to the fabric before cutting it out.

4 Fold your sole piece in half with the right sides of the fabric together. Sew up the heel edge with a running stitch, 1.5cm in from the edge (see page 20). Turn back and sew between the stitches already sewn. Tie a knot at the end and turn your fabric the right way around.

5 Place the middle of the toe piece against the middle of your sole piece at the toe end. With the edges together, from the middle point, join the top and bottom pieces by sewing towards the back of the shoe. Do this with a running stitch 1.5cm in from the edge. Stop when you meet the wider part of the sole piece.

6 Sew between the stitches already sewn and around to the other side. Turn back and finish back at the middle point. Knot the end.

7 Turn over the templates cut in steps 1 and 3 and cut material to make the other moccasin in the same way.

8 To decorate, cut a length of cord, thread on a bead and tie on a feather. Loop the cord around the heel and turn down the sides and front of the moccasin.

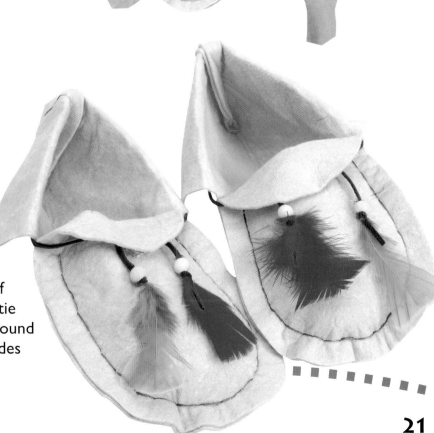

Glossary

dilute

To make a liquid weaker by mixing it with water.

heel

The part of a shoe or slipper below the back of the foot. Some shoes have hardly any heel while other shoes have very high heels.

kimono

The traditional silk dress worn by Japanese women.

kit

The special clothes and shoes that a person uses to play sport. For example, a football kit consists of a shirt, shorts, boots and shin pads.

Lapland

A region in northern Europe that covers part of Norway, Sweden, Finland and Russia.

material

Anything used for making something else. Leather, metal, wood and plastic are all materials.

Native Americans

The people who lived on the Great Plains area of North America. Native Americans were divided into several different tribes, including the Cheyenne and the Sioux.

North Pole

The most northerly point on the surface of Earth.

papier mâché

Paper that has been made into a pulp or layered with a glue and water mixture to make objects that are solid when dry.

petticoat

A thin skirt worn underneath a dress or skirt so that the dress or skirt is not see-through.

recycling

To recycle something is to change it or treat it so that it can be used again. For example, the metal in drinks cans can be recycled into other metal things.

reusing

To use something for a different purpose. For example, if you use the cardboard from a cereal packet to make a project, you are reusing the cardboard.

running stitch

A simple stitch where the thread is worked in and out of the fabric. The stitches can be short or long.

saree

The traditional dress worn by Indian women.

sole

The bottom part of a shoe between the ground and a person's foot. Trainers have thick soles and flip-flops usually have thin soles.

stud

The metal or plastic bit on the bottom of a shoe or boot. Studs on rugby boots and football boots help the shoes to grip the grass so that players do not slip when they run.

tabs

Flaps or small pieces that stick out of something.

template

A pattern.

traditional

Things that have existed for a long time or that have been passed down through families.

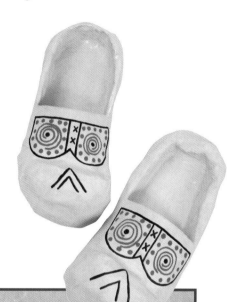

FURTHER INFORMATION

www.batashoemuseum.ca/collectindex.html
The Bata Shoe Museum in Canada has many shoes on display. Log on to their website to see their collection of shoes from around the world.
www.sherwoodsspirit.com/category/moccasins
This website has loads of pictures of different moccasins. It is great for inspiration for when you decorate yours.
www.metmuseum.org/toah/hd/shoe/hd_shoe.htm
This is the website for the Metropolitan Museum of Art, New York, USA. The Metropolitan Museum has a good collection of shoes and its website is packed with images of historical and modern shoes from The Costume Institute.

Note to parents and teachers:

The website addresses (URLs) included in this book were valid at the time of going to press. However, because of the nature of the Internet, it is possible that some addresses may have changed, or sites may have changed or closed down since publication. While the author and publishers regret any inconvenience this may cause the readers, no responsibility for any such changes can be accepted by either the author or the publisher.

Index